Best Friends

A play by Julia Donaldson

Illustrated by Marion Lindsay

Characters

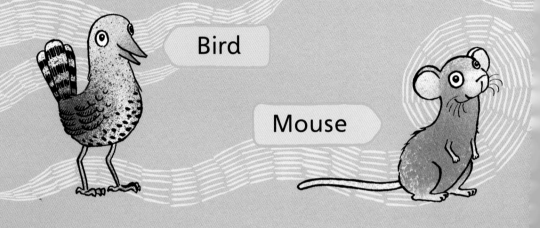

Bird

Mouse

Mountain

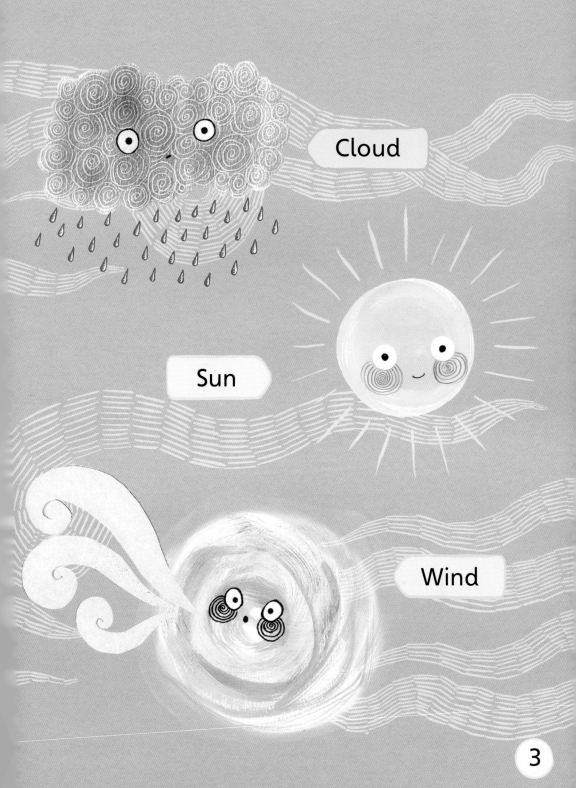

Cloud

Sun

Wind

3

Characters

Sun: I am the sun.

Cloud: I am a cloud.

Wind: I am the wind.

Mountain: I am a mountain.

Bird: I am a bird.

Mouse: And I am a mouse. We're best friends, aren't we, Bird?

Bird: I'll have to think about it.

Mouse: Why will you have to think about it, Bird?

Bird: Well, you are rather little and weak. I'd like to have a really strong best friend.

Mouse: Like who?

Bird: The sun. You're stronger than everyone, aren't you, Sun? You're so hot and bright.

Sun: Ah, but there's someone even stronger than me.

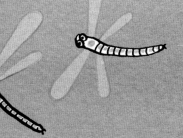

Bird: Who's stronger than Sun?

Wind: Who can it be?

Mountain: I can't think.

Sun: It's this big black cloud. When Cloud sits in front of me, no one can see me any more.

Bird: In that case, I'll ask the cloud to be my best friend.

q

Bird: How about it, Cloud? I hear you're stronger than everyone.

Cloud: That's not quite true. There's someone even stronger than me.

Bird: Who is it?

Mountain: I can't think.

Mouse: Who can it be?

Cloud: It's the wind. He's so strong he can blow me about all over the sky.

Bird: In that case, I'll ask the wind to be my best friend.

Bird: How about it, Wind? I hear you're the strongest one.

Wind: That's not quite true. There's someone even stronger than me.

Bird: Who is it?

Sun: Who can it be?

Cloud: I can't think.

Wind: It's the mountain. I just can't blow it down, however hard I try.

Bird: Then I'll ask the mountain to be my best friend.

13

Bird: How about it, Mountain? I've been hearing how strong you are.

Mountain: Ah, but there's someone even stronger than me.

Bird: Who is it?

Cloud: Who can it be?

Mouse: I can't think.

Mountain: Can't you?

Mouse: No, I can't.

Mountain: Well, it's you!

Mouse: Me?

Mountain: Yes. You keep nibbling holes in me, and there's nothing I can do to stop you.

Bird: So the little mouse is the strongest one of all! Shall we go back to being best friends, Mouse?

Mouse: I'll have to think about it!